Becoming an Eel

by Grace Hansen

CHANGING ANIMALS

Abdo
Kids

Abdo Kids Jumbo is an Imprint of Abdo Kids
abdopublishing.com

abdopublishing.com

Published by Abdo Kids, a division of ABDO, P.O. Box 398166, Minneapolis, Minnesota 55439.
Copyright © 2019 by Abdo Consulting Group, Inc. International copyrights reserved in all countries.
No part of this book may be reproduced in any form without written permission from the publisher.
Abdo Kids Jumbo™ is a trademark and logo of Abdo Kids.

052018

092018

Photo Credits: Alamy, Animals Animals, iStock, Minden Pictures, Science Source, Shutterstock

Production Contributors: Teddy Borth, Jennie Forsberg, Grace Hansen

Design Contributors: Dorothy Toth, Laura Mitchell

Library of Congress Control Number: 2017960562

Publisher's Cataloging-in-Publication Data

Names: Hansen, Grace, author.

Title: Becoming an eel / by Grace Hansen.

Description: Minneapolis, Minnesota : Abdo Kids, 2019. | Series: Changing animals |
    Includes glossary, index and online resources (page 24).

Identifiers: ISBN 9781532108198 (lib.bdg.) | ISBN 9781532109171 (ebook) |
    ISBN 9781532109669 (Read-to-me ebook)

Subjects: LCSH: Eels--Juvenile literature. | Animal life cycles--Juvenile literature. |
    Metamorphosis--Juvenile literature. | Animal behavior--Juvenile literature.

Classification: DDC 571.876--dc23

Table of Contents

Stage 1

Eels come in all shapes, sizes, and colors. Their lives can also be very different. Some spend their entire lives in the ocean. Others can live in both fresh and salt water.

American eels are freshwater eels. But they are born in the ocean. Female eels lay their eggs in the ocean. The eggs hatch within a week.

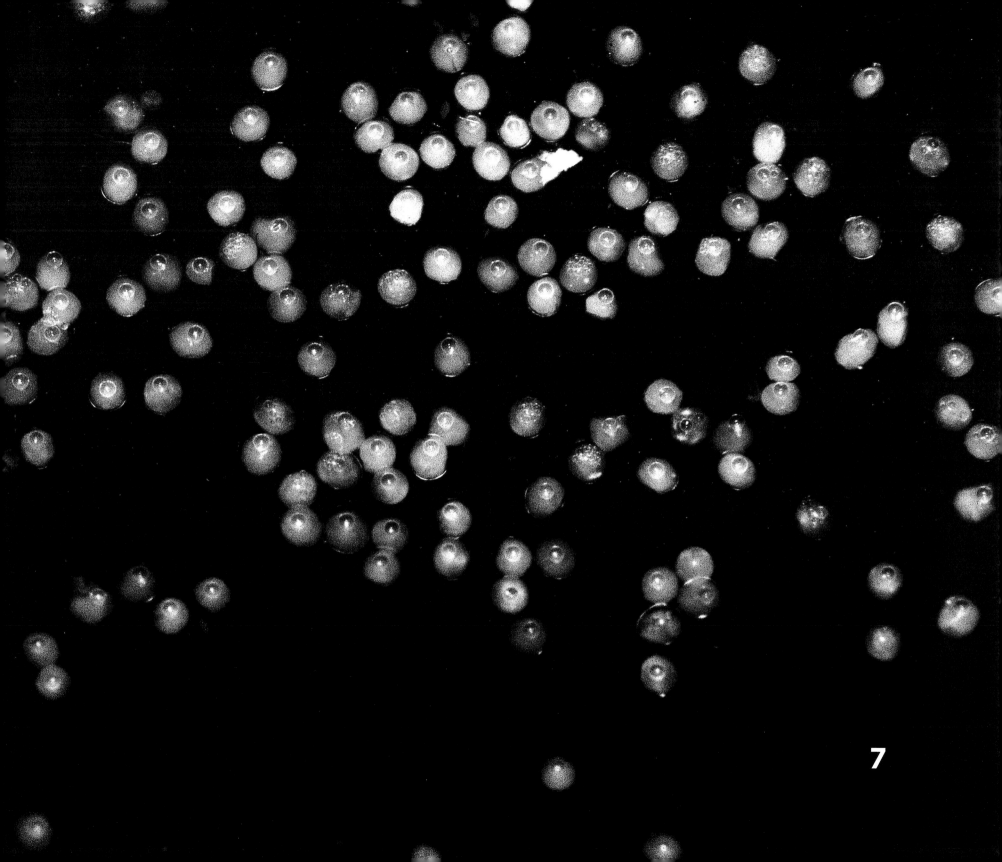

Stage 2

When an eel hatches it is a **larva**. It looks very different from an adult eel. Its body is flat and clear. It drifts with the ocean's **current**.

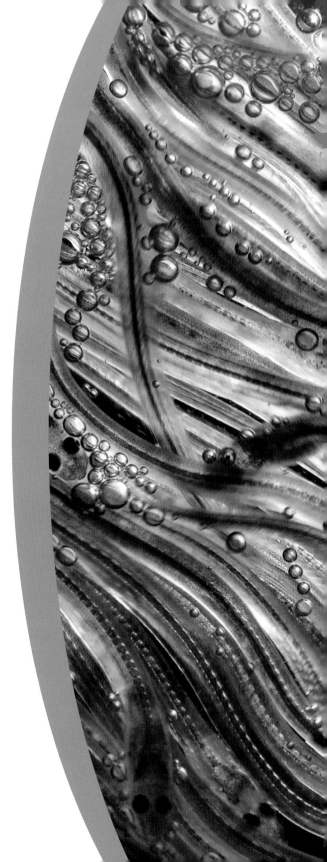

The **larva** drifts to the **coast**.

This takes about one year.

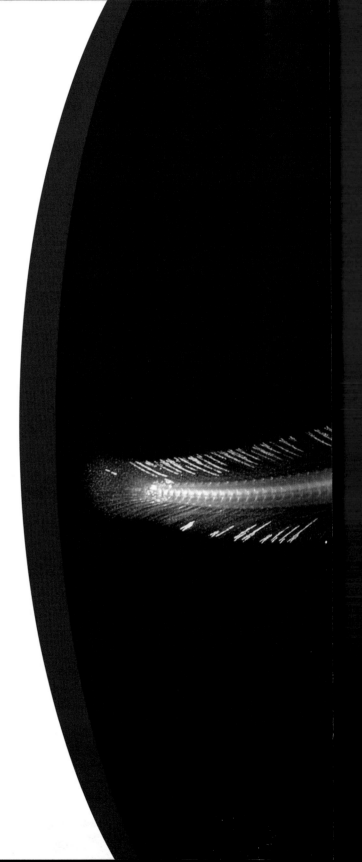

11

Stage 3

The eel now has fins. It is shaped like an adult. But its body is still clear. It is called a glass eel.

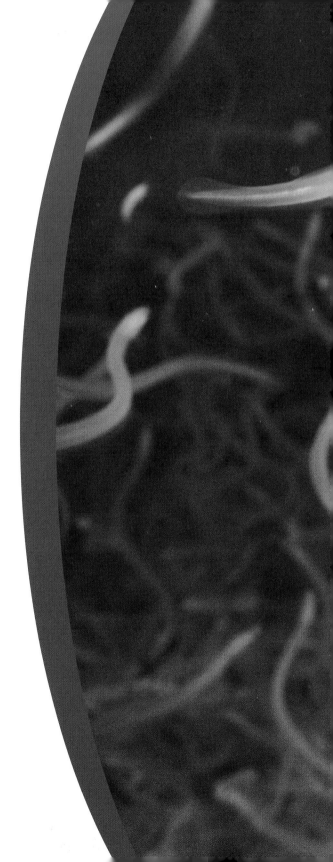

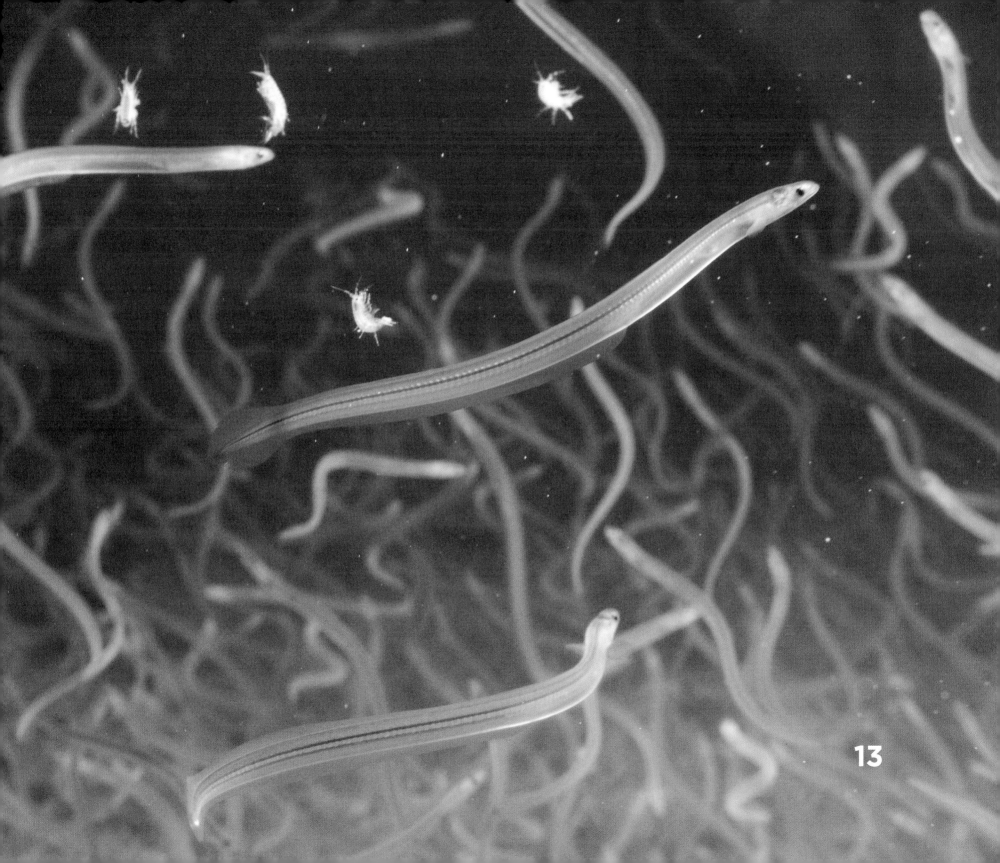

Stage 4

The eel grows at least 4 inches (10.2 cm) long. Its body turns gray, green, or brown. It is called an elver now.

15

Stage 5

Soon, the eel becomes a yellow eel. It is a **bottom dweller**. It hides under logs and rocks. It can live in fresh or **brackish** water.

16

Stage 6

After 3 to 4 years, the eel is an adult. It is called a silver eel now. Female American eels can grow to 5 feet (1.5 m) long. Males are often 3 feet (0.9 m) long.

19

Silver eels return to the sea. They go through more changes to be able to do this. There, females can release up to 30 million eggs!

More Facts

- Though they look like snakes, eels are fish!

- Yellow eels that stay in salt water grow faster than those that live in fresh water.

- Moray eels are a type of saltwater eel. Some can live in fresh water. Like freshwater eels, their larvae drift in the ocean for up to one year.

Glossary

bottom dweller – a fish that lives and feeds near the bottom of a body of water.

brackish – somewhat salty.

coast – land near the ocean.

current – water that flows in one direction.

freshwater – living in fresh water.

larva – the early form of an animal that at birth or hatching does not look like its parents and must grow and change to become an adult.

Index

Abdo Kids
ONLINE
FREE! ONLINE MULTIMEDIA RESOURCES

Visit **abdokids.com** and use this code to access crafts, games, videos, and more!

Abdo Kids Code:
CBK8198